To...

From.....................................

I'M NEVER
GOING TO FIND
SOMEONE AS
GOOD AS MY
MOTHER, AM I?

Justin Timberlake

I love my mother as the trees love water and sunshine – she helps me grow, prosper and reach great heights.

Terri Guillemets

GOD COULD NOT BE EVERYWHERE, SO HE CREATED MOTHERS.

Jewish proverb

"

Mothers... carry the
key of our souls in
their bosoms.

OLIVER WENDELL HOLMES SR

"

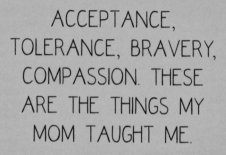

ACCEPTANCE,
TOLERANCE, BRAVERY,
COMPASSION. THESE
ARE THE THINGS MY
MOM TAUGHT ME.

- LADY GAGA -

"

MOTHERS ARE
THE HEART OF
ANY HOUSEHOLD.

- HELENA BONHAM
CARTER -

THERE WAS
NEVER A GREAT
MAN WHO HAD
NOT A GREAT
MOTHER.

Olive Schreiner

EVERYTHING
I AM, YOU HELPED
ME TO BE.

YOU WILL
ALWAYS BE
YOUR CHILD'S
FAVOURITE TOY.

Vicki Lansky

I know enough to know
that when you're in a
pickle... call mom.

Jennifer Garner

*I hope they're
still making women
like my mama.*

JOE LOUIS

"

A MOTHER IS THE TRUEST FRIEND WE HAVE.

- WASHINGTON IRVING -

"

IF EVOLUTION REALLY
WORKS, HOW COME
MOTHERS ONLY HAVE
TWO HANDS?

Milton Berle

Keep love in your heart...
The consciousness of loving
and being loved brings a
warmth and richness to life
that nothing else can bring.

Oscar Wilde

**I hope you know how
incredible you are.**

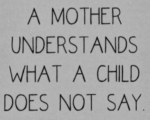

A MOTHER
UNDERSTANDS
WHAT A CHILD
DOES NOT SAY.

- ANONYMOUS -

MOTHERHOOD: ALL LOVE BEGINS AND ENDS THERE.

Robert Browning

THE MOST IMPORTANT THINGS IN LIFE AREN'T THINGS.

Anthony J. D'Angelo

BIOLOGY IS
THE LEAST OF
WHAT MAKES
SOMEONE A
MOTHER.

Oprah Winfrey

My mother had a slender, small body, but a large heart — a heart so large that everybody's joys found welcome in it, and hospitable accommodation.

Mark Twain

"

THE MOMENT A
CHILD IS BORN,
THE MOTHER IS
ALSO BORN.

- OSHO -

"

To describe my mother
would be to write about
a hurricane in its
perfect power.

Maya Angelou

"

My mother is the bones of my spine, keeping me straight and true.

KRISTIN HANNAH

"

MOTHERHOOD IS THE GREATEST THING AND THE HARDEST THING.

Ricki Lake

A MOTHER ALWAYS
HAS TO THINK
TWICE: ONCE FOR
HERSELF AND ONCE
FOR HER CHILD.

Sophia Loren

WHEN A CHILD
NEEDS A MOTHER
TO TALK TO,
NOBODY ELSE
BUT A MOTHER
WILL DO.

Erica Jong

THERE IS SUCH A
SPECIAL SWEETNESS
IN BEING ABLE TO
PARTICIPATE IN
CREATION.

- PAMELA S. NADAV -

All motherly love
is really without
reason and logic.

Joan Chen

MOTHERS HOLD
THEIR CHILDREN'S
HANDS FOR A SHORT
WHILE, BUT THEIR
HEARTS FOREVER.

Anonymous

YOU INSPIRE ME EVERY DAY.

I can only hope to be
ten per cent of the mom
mine was to me. She
encouraged me to be
confident and enjoy life.

Charlize Theron

"

MEN ARE WHAT THEIR MOTHERS MADE THEM.

- RALPH WALDO EMERSON -

"

SUCCESSFUL MOTHERS
ARE NOT THE ONES
THAT HAVE NEVER
STRUGGLED. THEY ARE
THE ONES THAT NEVER
GIVE UP, DESPITE
THE STRUGGLES.

- SHARON JAYNES -

CHILDREN ARE THE ANCHORS OF A MOTHER'S LIFE.

Sophocles

When you look
at your mother, you
are looking at the
purest love you
will ever know.

MITCH ALBOM

BECOMING A MOTHER
MAKES YOU REALIZE
YOU CAN DO ALMOST
ANYTHING ONE-HANDED.

- ANONYMOUS -

THAT BEST
ACADEMY, A
MOTHER'S
KNEE.

James Russell Lowell

Anyone who doesn't
miss the past never
had a mother.

Gregory Nunn

Thank you for teaching me you can be both strong and gentle.

Mother is the one
we count on for the
things that matter
most of all.

KATHARINE BUTLER HATHAWAY

Mother's love is
bliss, is peace, it need
not be acquired, it need
not be deserved.

Erich Fromm

Who is it that loves
me and will love me
forever with an affection
which no chance, no
misery, no crime of
mine can do away?
It is you, my mother.

Thomas Carlyle

TO A CHILD'S EAR,
"MOTHER" IS MAGIC IN
ANY LANGUAGE.

- ARLENE BENEDICT -

THERE'S NO WAY TO
BE A PERFECT MOTHER
AND A MILLION WAYS
TO BE A GOOD ONE.

Jill Churchill

"

THERE IS NO
LOVE AS PURE,
UNCONDITIONAL
AND STRONG AS A
MOTHER'S LOVE.

- HOPE EDELMAN -

"

YOU ALWAYS KNOW EXACTLY WHAT TO SAY.

MOTHER – THAT WAS THE BANK WHERE WE DEPOSITED ALL OUR HURTS AND WORRIES.

- THOMAS DE WITT TALMAGE -

MOTHER IS THE
NAME OF GOD
IN THE LIPS
AND HEARTS
OF LITTLE
CHILDREN.

William Makepeace Thackeray

Motherhood has a very humanizing effect. Everything gets reduced to essentials.

MERYL STREEP

MOST MOTHERS
ARE INSTINCTIVE
PHILOSOPHERS.

Harriet Beecher Stowe

THERE IS NO
ROLE IN LIFE MORE
ESSENTIAL AND MORE
ETERNAL THAN THAT
OF MOTHERHOOD.

- M. RUSSELL BALLARD -

She never quite leaves
her children at home,
even when she doesn't
take them along.

Margaret Culkin Banning

LOVE IS WHAT
MAKES YOU
SMILE WHEN
YOU ARE TIRED.

Paulo Coelho

SHE REJOICED AS
ONLY MOTHERS
CAN IN THE GOOD
FORTUNES OF
THEIR CHILDREN.

Louisa May Alcott

YOU'RE ALWAYS
THERE FOR ME –
NO MATTER WHAT!

Beautiful as was
mamma's face, it became
incomparably more
lovely when she smiled,
and seemed to enliven
everything about her.

Leo Tolstoy

A MOTHER IS
ONE TO WHOM YOU
HURRY WHEN YOU
ARE TROUBLED.

- EMILY DICKINSON -

"

THE RAISING OF A CHILD IS THE BUILDING OF A CATHEDRAL. YOU CAN'T CUT CORNERS.

- DAVE EGGERS -

"

If love is sweet as a
flower, then my mother is
that sweet flower of love.

Stevie Wonder

I believe the choice to become a mother is the choice to become one of the greatest spiritual teachers there is.

OPRAH WINFREY

MUM ALWAYS SAYS THE RIGHT THING. SHE ALWAYS MAKES EVERYTHING BETTER.

Sophie Kinsella

I CAN'T
IMAGINE
A BETTER
M♥M THAN
YOU.

A SMART MOTHER
MAKES OFTEN A
BETTER DIAGNOSIS
THAN A POOR
DOCTOR.

- AUGUST BIER -

MOTHERHOOD
IS HEART-
EXPLODING,
BLISSFUL
HYSTERIA.

Olivia Wilde

WE ARE BORN OF LOVE; LOVE IS OUR MOTHER.

Rumi

BEING A MOTHER
IS HARD AND IT
WASN'T A SUBJECT
I EVER STUDIED.

Ruby Wax

"

MY MOTHER IS THE MOST SUPPORTIVE MOTHER IN THE WORLD – SHE'S MAGICAL.

"

- VIN DIESEL -

"

*I know that is what
I was put on Earth to
do – to be a mother.*

CHERYL

"

We never know the love
of a parent till we become
parents ourselves.

Henry Ward Beecher

WHERE THERE IS A
MOTHER IN THE HOME,
MATTERS GO WELL.

- AMOS BRONSON ALCOTT -

You're my
favourite person.

"

WHAT IS DONE
WITH LOVE IS
DONE WELL.

- VINCENT VAN GOGH -

"

FOR WE THINK
BACK THROUGH
OUR MOTHERS IF
WE ARE WOMEN.

Virginia Woolf

You make sacrifices
to become a mother, but
you really find yourself
and your soul.

Mariska Hargitay

FAMILY IS NOT
AN IMPORTANT
THING. IT'S
EVERYTHING.

Michael J. Fox

A father's goodness is
higher than the mountain,
a mother's goodness
deeper than the sea.

Japanese proverb

Of all the roles I've played, none has been as fulfilling as being a mother.

ANNETTE FUNICELLO

YOU'RE A M♡M
IN A MILLION.

HAVING CHILDREN
JUST PUTS THE
WHOLE WORLD
INTO PERSPECTIVE.
EVERYTHING ELSE
JUST DISAPPEARS.

- KATE WINSLET -

Mothers and their children are in a category all their own. There's no bond so strong in the entire world.

Gail Tsukiyama

A MOTHER IS THE ONE WHO FILLS YOUR HEART IN THE FIRST PLACE.

Amy Tan

Motherhood is a choice
you make every day,
to put someone else's
happiness and well-being
ahead of your own.

Donna Ball

" "

RAISING KIDS IS
PART JOY AND
PART GUERRILLA
WARFARE.

" "

- ED ASNER -

SING OUT LOUD
IN THE CAR EVEN,
OR ESPECIALLY, IF
IT EMBARRASSES
YOUR CHILDREN.

- MARILYN PENLAND -

ONE GOOD MOTHER IS WORTH A HUNDRED SCHOOLMASTERS.

George Herbert

MOTHERHOOD
IN ALL ITS
GUISES AND
PERMUTATIONS
IS MORE ART
THAN SCIENCE.

Melinda M. Marshall

**A mother's hug is like
a warm cup of tea on
a rainy day.**

A good mother is irreplaceable.

ADRIANA TRIGIANI

Mother is the heartbeat
in the home; and without
her, there seems to be
no heart throb.

Leroy Brownlow

OTHER THINGS
MAY CHANGE US, BUT
WE START AND END
WITH FAMILY.

Anthony Brandt

My mother made a
brilliant impression upon
my childhood life. She
shone for me like the
evening star.

Winston Churchill

A mother is not a person to lean on, but a person to make leaning unnecessary.

Dorothy Canfield Fisher

"

A MOTHER'S
ARMS ARE MORE
COMFORTING THAN
ANYONE ELSE'S.

- DIANA,
  PRINCESS OF WALES -

YOU
KNOW ME
BETTER
THAN
ANYONE
ELSE.

MY MOTHER HAD
A GREAT DEAL OF
TROUBLE WITH ME,
BUT I THINK SHE
ENJOYED IT.

- MARK TWAIN -

THERE IS ONLY
ONE PRETTY
CHILD IN THE
WORLD, AND
EVERY MOTHER
HAS IT.

Chinese proverb

There is a point at which
you aren't so much mom
and daughter as you are
adults and friends.

Jamie Lee Curtis

No influence is so powerful as that of the mother.

SARAH JOSEPHA HALE

I GOT MY FIGURE
BACK AFTER GIVING
BIRTH. SAD, I'D
HOPED TO GET
SOMEBODY ELSE'S.

Caroline Quentin

IT SEEMS TO ME
THAT MY MOTHER
WAS THE MOST
SPLENDID WOMAN
I EVER KNEW.

- CHARLIE CHAPLIN -

A MOTHER'S LOVE FOR HER CHILD IS LIKE NOTHING ELSE IN THE WORLD.

Agatha Christie

THE BEST
WAY TO MAKE
CHILDREN
GOOD IS TO
MAKE THEM
HAPPY.

Oscar Wilde

I'M SO PROUD
TO CALL YOU
MY M♥M.

Before I got married,
I had six theories about
bringing up children; now
I have six children and
no theories.

John Wilmot, 2nd Earl of Rochester

A SUBURBAN
MOTHER'S ROLE IS
TO DELIVER CHILDREN
OBSTETRICALLY
ONCE, AND BY CAR
FOREVER AFTER.

- PETER DE VRIES -

MY MOTHER
IS A WALKING
MIRACLE.

Leonardo DiCaprio

A little girl, asked where her home was, replied: "Where mother is."

Keith L. Brooks

"

Blessed is a mother that would give up part of her soul for her children's happiness.

SHANNON L. ALDER

"

Pregnancy and motherhood are the most beautiful and significantly life-altering events that I have ever experienced.

Elisabeth Hasselbeck

**I can't imagine life
without you – literally!**

THERE IS
NOTHING AS
SINCERE AS A
MOTHER'S KISS.

Saleem Sharma

THE DAUGHTER
PRAYS; THE
MOTHER LISTENS.

Amanda Downum

I CAN IMAGINE NO
HEROISM GREATER
THAN MOTHERHOOD.

Lance Conrad

*A boy's best friend
is his mother.*

JOSEPH STEFANO

MOTHERS POSSESS A POWER BEYOND THAT OF A KING ON HIS THRONE.

- MABEL HALE -

Our mothers always remain
the strangest, craziest
people we've ever met.

Marguerite Duras

HEAVEN IS AT THE FEET OF MOTHERS.

Arabic proverb

I WONDERED IF
MY SMILE WAS AS
BIG AS HERS. MAYBE
AS BIG. BUT NOT
AS BEAUTIFUL.

-BENJAMIN ALIRE SÁENZ,
ON HIS MOTHER -

M♥m is just another word for home.

IF YOU KNEW HOW
GREAT IS A MOTHER'S
LOVE, YOU WOULD
HAVE NO FEAR.

J. M. Barrie

THERE IS A POWER THAT COMES TO WOMEN WHEN THEY GIVE BIRTH.

Sheryl Feldman

A mother's arms are made
of tenderness and children
sleep soundly in them.

Victor Hugo

SWEATER, N:
GARMENT WORN
BY CHILD WHEN
ITS MOTHER IS
FEELING CHILLY.

- AMBROSE BIERCE -

Children keep us
in check. Their laughter
prevents our hearts
from hardening.

Queen Rania of Jordan

Being a full-time mother
is one of the highest
salaried jobs... since the
payment is pure love.

Mildred B. Vermont

THERE'S NOTHING
LIKE TIME SPENT
WITH M♡M.

66

The art of mothering
is to teach the art of
living to children.

ELAINE HEFFNER

99

> **MOTHER WAS COMFORT. MOTHER WAS HOME.**
>
> - RUTA SEPETYS -

MY MOTHER HAS
ALWAYS BEEN
MY EMOTIONAL
BAROMETER AND
MY GUIDANCE.

Emma Stone

IN A CHILD'S
EYES, A
MOTHER IS
A GODDESS.

N. K. Jemisin

THERE'S NOTHING
LIKE A MAMA-HUG.

Terri Guillemets

The successful mother
sets her children free and
becomes more free herself
in the process.

Robert J. Havighurst

TO BE DEEPLY
LOVED BY SOMEONE
GIVES YOU STRENGTH,
BUT TO LOVE SOMEONE
DEEPLY GIVES YOU
COURAGE.

- ESTHER HUERTAS -

SHE MAY SCOLD
YOU FOR LITTLE
THINGS, BUT
NEVER FOR THE
BIG ONES.

Harry S. Truman

**You're
m♥m-believable!**

Love is a great beautifier.

LOUISA MAY ALCOTT

The most beautiful word on the lips of mankind is the word "Mother".

Kahlil Gibran

I thought my mom's whole purpose was to be my mom. That's how she made me feel.

Natasha Gregson Wagner

ALL MOTHERS
ARE RICH WHEN
THEY LOVE THEIR
CHILDREN.

Maurice Maeterlinck

I CANNOT TELL YOU
HOW MUCH I OWE TO
THE SOLEMN WORD OF
MY GOOD MOTHER.

- CHARLES SPURGEON -

It is to decide forever to have your heart go walking around outside your body.

Elizabeth Stone,
on making the decision
to have a child

THANK YOU FOR
ALWAYS BEING
SO PATIENT.

The best and most beautiful
things... cannot be seen or
even touched. They must
be felt with the heart.

Helen Keller

"

LIFE BEGAN
WITH WAKING UP
AND LOVING MY
MOTHER'S FACE.

- GEORGE ELIOT -

"

No language can express
the power, and beauty,
and heroism, and majesty
of a mother's love.

Edwin H. Chapin

CHILDREN ARE
NOT A DISTRACTION
FROM MORE
IMPORTANT WORK.
THEY ARE THE MOST
IMPORTANT WORK.

- JOHN TRAINER -

MY MOTHER... SHE IS BEAUTIFUL, SOFTENED AT THE EDGES AND TEMPERED WITH A SPINE OF STEEL.

Jodi Picoult

> *All that I am my mother made me.*
>
> JOHN QUINCY ADAMS

66

SOMETIMES THE
STRENGTH OF
MOTHERHOOD IS
GREATER THAN
NATURAL LAWS.

- BARBARA KINGSOLVER -

99

I want my children to have all the things I couldn't afford. Then I want to move in with them.

Phyllis Diller

YOU BRING OUT THE BEST IN ME.

Mothers are endowed
with a love that is unlike
any other love on the
face of the earth.

Marjorie Pay Hinckley

CHILDREN AND
MOTHERS NEVER TRULY
PART – BOUND IN THE
BEATING OF EACH
OTHER'S HEARTS.

– CHARLOTTE GRAY –

She was the best
of all mothers, to whom,
for body and soul I owe
endless gratitude.

Thomas Carlyle

**You're by far the
world's best m♥m!**

If you're interested in finding out
more about our books, find us on Facebook
at Summersdale Publishers and follow us
on Twitter at @Summersdale.

www.summersdale.com

Image credits

pp.6, 8, 16, 18, 19, 21, 28, 31, 33, 37, 38, 40, 43,
47, 48, 51, 54, 55, 61, 65, 67, 70, 74, 75, 77, 83, 85,
88, 91, 94, 103, 104, 109, 113, 114, 117, 122, 123,
124, 127, 135, 137, 139, 143, 144, 150, 151, 157,
159 © Ps_Ai/Shutterstock.com